Gran's hat

Gran sat.
The cat sat, the rat sat and the bat sat on Gran's mat.

Gran sat and sat and sat
and … zzzzz … zzzzz …

Jack's big fat cat sat.

Jack's fat cat
sat on Gran's hat,

on Gran's big flat hat!

Big fat rat sat.

Big fat rat
sat on Jack's fat cat,

and Jack's fat cat

sat on Gran's big flat hat!

Big fat bat sat.

Big fat bat
sat on big fat rat

and big fat rat
sat on Jack's fat cat

and Jack's fat cat

sat on Gran's big flat hat!

Up sat Gran! No flat hat!

No big fat cat,
no big fat rat,
and no big fat bat
on Gran's hat.